GO HANG A SALAMI! I'M A LASAGNA HOG!

GO HANG A SALAMI!

I'M A LASAGNA HOG!

and Other Palindromes by JON AGEE

Farrar · Straus · Giroux   New York

To Hannah

Copyright © 1991 by Jon Agee. All rights reserved
Library of Congress catalog card number: 91-31319
Published in Canada by HarperCollins*CanadaLtd*
Printed and bound in the United States of America
First edition, 1991
Third printing, 1994

TAHITI HAT

SALT AN
ATLAS

SMART RAMS

NEIL, AN ALIEN

LAST EGG GETS AL

A CAR, A MAN, A MARACA

EMIL'S NIECE, IN SLIME

ED IS ON NO SIDE

SUB'S KNOB BONKS BUS

EMILY'S SASSY LIME

DROWSY SWORD

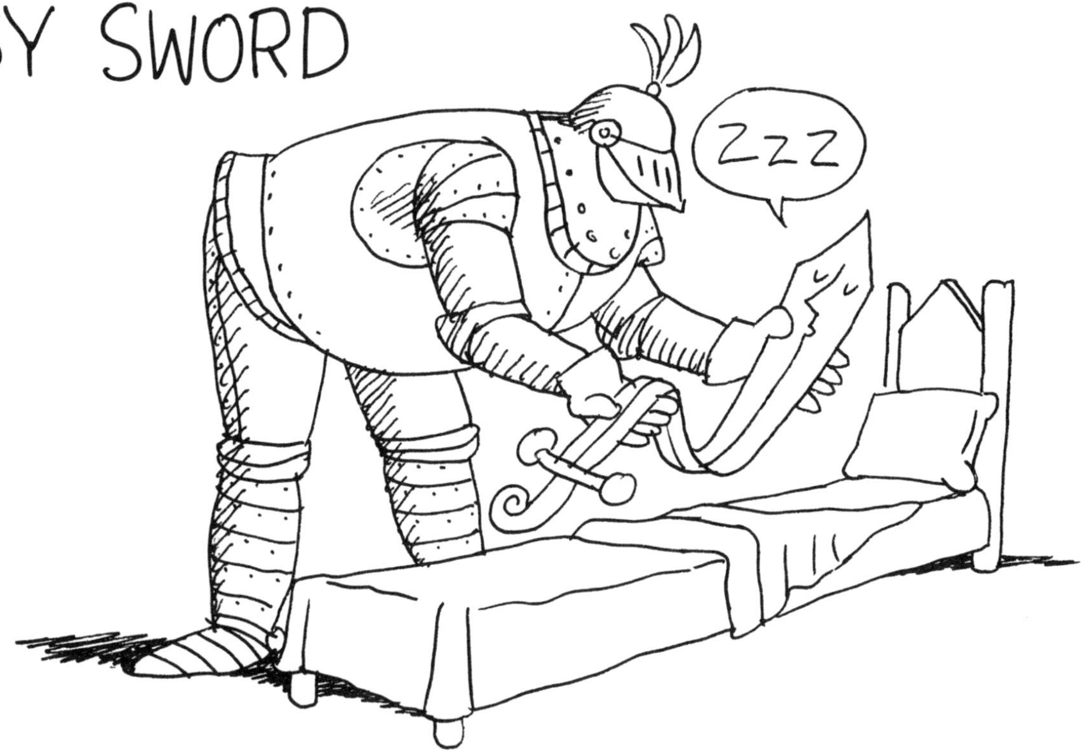

POOH'S HOOP

DAMON,
A NOMAD

MAC SNUBS
BOB'S BUN SCAM

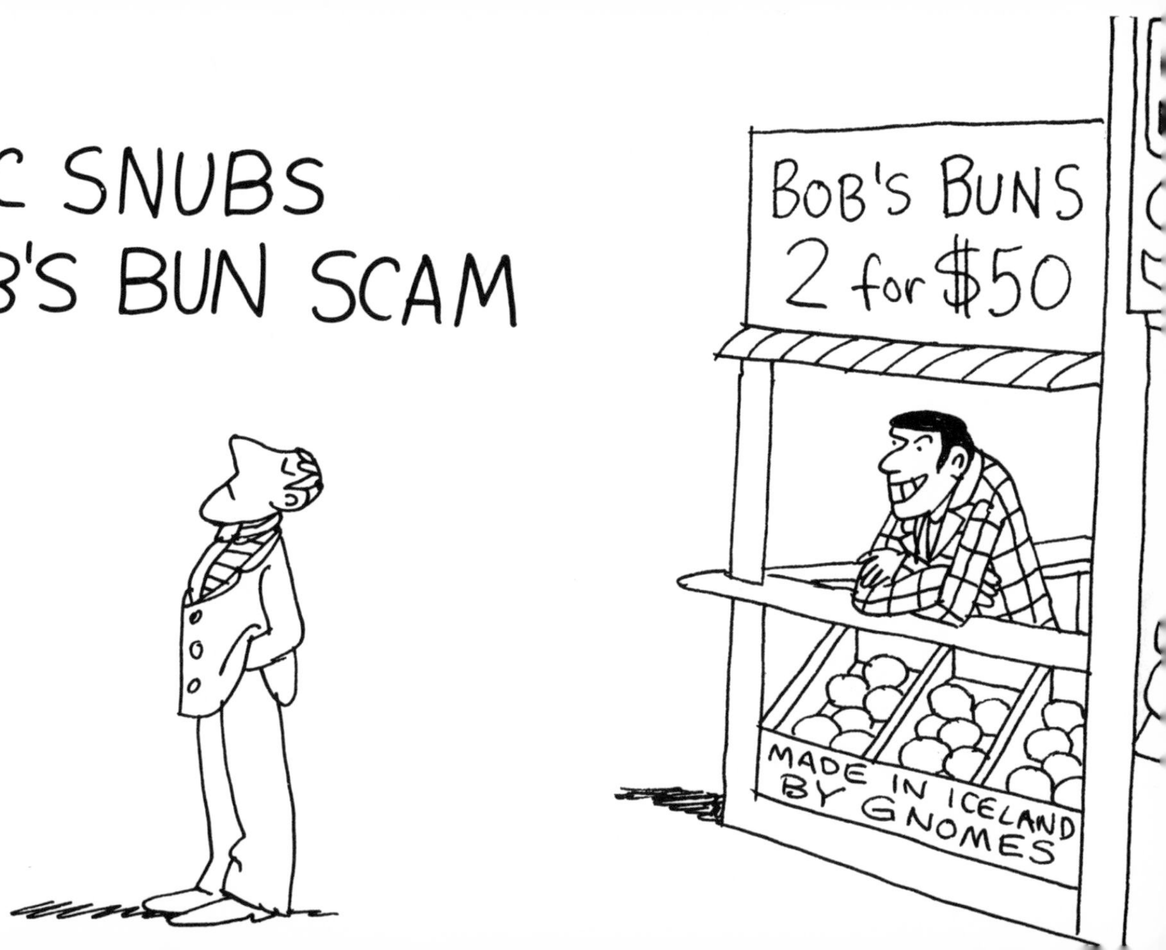

SNUG
LI'L GUNS

OOZY RAT
IN A SANITARY ZOO

Thanks to

Dan Allen, Tom Bassmann, John Baumann,
Russell Busch, Dan Feigelson, Holly McGhee,
Phil Warton, Maria Warton-Bennett and
Stephen Wolf for their contributions.

Racecar Level DAD r

KOOK SIS deed

KAYAK Civic Madam

Otto Stats Bob ANNA de

reviver DUD